GERMAN

Made Nice & Easy!®

Staff of Research & Education Association
Carl Fuchs, Language Program Director

Based on Language Courses developed by the
U.S. Government for Foreign Service Personnel

Research & Education Association
61 Ethel Road West
Piscataway, New Jersey 08854

Dr. M. Fogiel, Director

GERMAN MADE NICE & EASY®

Year 2003 Printing

Printed in the United States of America

Library of Congress Control Number 00-193024

International Standard Book Number 0-87891-369-6

What This Guide Will Do For You

Whether travelling to a foreign country or to your favorite international restaurant, this *Nice & Easy* guide gives you just enough of the language to get around and be understood. Much of the material in this book was developed for government personnel who are often assigned to a foreign country on a moment's notice and need a quick introduction to the language.

In this handy and compact guide, you will find useful words and phrases, popular expressions, common greetings, and the words for numbers, money, and time. Every word or phrase is accompanied with the correct pronunciation and spelling. There is a vocabulary list for finding words quickly.

Generous margins on the pages allow you to make notes and remarks that you may find helpful.

If you expect to travel to Germany, the section on the country's history and relevant up-to-date facts will make your trip more informative and enjoyable. By keeping this guide with you, you'll be well prepared to understand as well as converse in German.

Carl Fuchs
Language Program Director

Contents

GERMANY

FACTS & HISTORY

Official Name: Federal Republic of Germany

Geography
Area: 357,000 sq. km. (137,821 sq. mi.); about the size of Montana.
Cities: *Capital*—Berlin (population about 3.5 million). *Other cities*—Hamburg (1.7 million), Munich (1.2 million), Cologne (964,000), Frankfurt (647,000), Essen (612,000), Dortmund (597,000), Stuttgart (585,000), Dusseldorf (571,000), Bremen (549,000), Hannover (523,000).
Terrain: Low plain in the north; high plains, hills, and basins in the center and east; mountainous alpine region in the south.
Climate: Temperate; cooler and rainier than much of the U.S.

People
Nationality: *Noun and adjective*—German(s).
Population: 82 million.
Ethnic groups: Primarily German; Danish minority in the north, Sorbian (Slavic) minority in the east, 7.3

million noncitizens.

Religions: Protestants slightly outnumber Roman Catholics.

Language: German.

Education: *Years compulsory*—10. *Attendance*—100%. *Literacy*—99%.

Health: *Infant mortality rate*—5.2/1,000. *Life expectancy*: Women 80 yrs., men 74 yrs.

Persons employed: 34.1 million.

Persons unemployed: 4.5 million—11.6% of labor force.

Government

Type: Federal republic.

Founded: 1949 (Basic Law, i.e., constitution, promulgated on May 23, 1949). On October 3, 1990, the Federal Republic of Germany and the German Democratic Republic unified in accordance with Article 23 of the F.R.G. Basic Law.

Branches: *Executive*—president (titular chief of state), chancellor (executive head of government). *Legislative*—bicameral parliament. *Judicial*—independent, Federal Constitutional Court.

Administrative divisions: 16 Laender (states).

Major political parties: Social Democratic Party (SPD); Christian Democratic Union (CDU); Christian Social Union (CSU); Alliance 90/Greens; Free Democratic Party (FDP); Party of Democratic Socialism (PDS).

Modern Germany

The population of Germany is primarily German. There are more than 7 million foreign residents, including those granted asylum, guest workers, and their dependents. Germany is a prime destination for political and economic refugees from many developing countries. An ethnic Danish minority lives in the north, and a small Slavic minority, known as the Sorbs, lives in eastern Germany.

Germany has one of the world's highest levels of education, technological development, and economic productivity. Since the end of World War II, the number of youths entering universities has more than tripled, and the trade and technical schools of the Federal Republic of Germany (F.R.G.) are among the world's best. With a per capita income level of more than $25,000, Germany is a broadly middle class society. A generous social welfare system provides for universal medical care, unemployment compensation, and other social needs. Germans also are mobile; millions travel abroad each year.

With unification on October 3, 1990, Germany began the major task of bringing the standard of living of Germans in the former German Democratic Republic (G.D.R.) up to that of western Germany. This continues to be a difficult process due to the relative inefficiency of industrial enterprises in the former G.D.R., difficulties in resolving property ownership in eastern Germany, and the inadequate infrastructure and environmental damage that resulted from years of mismanagement under communist rule.

Drastic changes in the socioeconomic landscape brought about by reunification have resulted in troubling social problems. Economic uncertainty in eastern Germany is often cited as one factor contributing to extremist violence, primarily from the political right. Confusion about the causes of the current hardships and a need to place blame have found expression in harassment and violence by some Germans directed toward foreigners, particularly non-Europeans. The vast majority of Germans condemn such violence.

History of Germany

Milestones in German History

800 - Charlemagne crowned emperor in Rome

843 - Under the Treaty of Verdun, Charlemagne's grandchildren divided up the empire: Lothar received the central, Charles the Bold the western, and Ludwig the German the eastern territories.

919 -The Saxon Duke, Henry I, was elected king. The Saxon dynasty ruled Germany until 1024

962 - Otto I was crowned Emperor in Rome and was recognized by Byzantium

1096 - Beginning of the first Crusade

1235 - Emperor Frederick II proclaimed the Peace of Mainz, the first imperial law in the German language.

1273 - Rudolf of Hapsburg became king of Germany. He increased power by his victory over King Ottocar II of Bohemia

1348 - The founding of the first German university in Prague, which Charles IV made the permanent capital of the empire

1348-1352 - The Plague ("black death")

1452 - Last coronation of a German emperor in Rome (Frederick III)

1517 - Luther proclaimed his 95 theses; beginning of the Reformation

1529 - The Turks laid siege to Vienna

1618 - A protest by Bohemian Protestants in Prague marked the beginning of the Thirty Years War

1697 - Prince August the Strong of Saxony became King of Poland

1701 - The elector Frederick III of Brandenburg crowned himself King Frederick I of Prussia in Koenigsberg

1756-1763 - The Seven-Year War (Prussia against Austria, France, Russia, Sweden and most of the imperial electors). The peace of Hubertusburg (1763) established the Dualism of Prussia and Austria

1792 - Beginning of the war against revolutionary France

1806 - Dissolution of the Holy Roman Empire of the German Nation

1813-1815 - Liberation wars against Napoleonic France

1815 - Founding of the German Confederation

1848 - Revolution in Germany; Frankfurt National Assembly Dissolution of the Prussian National Assembly, granting of a constitution

1849 - Campaign for a constitution for the Reich; uprisings in Saxony, Breslau and Baden were violently repressed

1862 - Bismarck became Prime Minister of Prussia

1866 - War between Prussia and Austria; dissolution of the German Confederation

1870-1871 - Franco-German War

1871 - Founding of the German Empire with Bismarck as Reich Chancellor; Coronation of Emperor William I in Versailles

1882 - Tripartite alliance with Austria and Italy

1890 - Dismissal of Bismarck

1914 - Outbreak of World War I

1919 - Peace Treaty of Versailles

1923 - Raging inflation; attempted coups by right-wing and left-wing radical groups

1925 - Hindenburg elected Reich President

1933 - Hitler became Reich Chancellor

1935 - Anti-Jewish "Nuremberg Laws"

1939 - German-Soviet Union non-agression pact; Germany's attack on Poland, beginning of World War II

1942 - Wannsee Conference (Nazi leadership decides to systematically eradicate European Jewry)

1945 - Hitler's suicide; unconditional surrender and occupation of Germany

1948 - End of Allied administration; separate currency reforms in East and West Germany

1948-1949 - Blockade of West Berlin by the Soviet Union; Berlin Airlift

1949 - Founding of the Federal Republic of Germany and the German Democratic Republic

1955 - Accession of the Federal Republic of Germany to NATO and of the GDR to the Warsaw Pact

1961 - The government of East Germany builds the Berlin Wall

1968 - Student unrest and "extra-parliamentary opposition" in the Federal Republic of Germany

1969-1974 - Willy Brandt is Federal Chancellor

1973 - East and West Germany become members of the United Nations

1974-1982 - Helmut Schmidt is Federal Chancellor

1990 - Unification Treaty between the Federal Republic of Germany and the GDR is signed in Berlin

1991 - German Parliament elects Helmut Kohl Federal Chancellor of unified Germany

1999 - Introduction of the EURO for non-cash transactions betweeen 11 participating European countries. Euro bills and coins to be introduced in the year 2002

The rise of Prussian power in the 19th century, supported by growing German nationalism, eventually ended interstate fighting and resulted in the formation of the German empire in 1871 under the chancellorship of Otto von Bismarck. Although authoritarian in many respects, the empire eventually permitted the development of political parties, and Bismarck was credited with passing the most advanced social welfare legislation of the age. Dynamic expansion of military power, however, contributed to tensions on the continent. The fragile European balance of power broke down in 1914, and World War I and its aftermath, including the Treaty of Versailles, led to the collapse of the German empire.

Fascism's Rise and Defeat

The postwar Weimar Republic (1919-33) was an attempt to establish a peaceful, liberal democratic regime in Germany. This government was severely handicapped and eventually doomed by economic problems and the inherent weakness of the Weimar state. The inflation of the early 1920s, the world depression of the 1930s, and the social unrest stemming from the draconian conditions of the Versailles Treaty worked to destroy the Weimar government from inside and out.

The National Socialist (Nazi) Party, led by Adolf Hitler, stressed nationalistic themes and promised to put the unemployed back to work. The party blamed many of Germany's ills on alleged Jewish conspiracies. Nazi support expanded rapidly in the early 1930s. Hitler was asked to form a government as Reich Chancellor in January 1933. After President Paul von Hindenburg died in 1934, Hitler assumed that office as well. Once in power, Hitler and his party first undermined then abolished democratic institutions and opposition parties. The Nazi leadership attempted to remove or subjugate the Jewish population in Germany and later, in the occupied countries, forced emigration and, ultimately, committed genocide. Hitler restored Germany's economic and military strength, but his ambitions led Germany into World War II. For Germany, World War II resulted in the destruction of its political and economic infrastructures, led to its division, and left a humiliating legacy.

After Germany's unconditional surrender on May 8, 1945, the United States, the United Kingdom, and the U.S.S.R. occupied the country and assumed responsibility for its administration. The commanders in chief exercised supreme authority in their respective zones and acted in concert on questions affecting the whole country. France was later given a separate zone of occupation.

Although the United States, the United Kingdom, and the Soviet Union agreed at Potsdam in August 1945 to a broad program of decentralization, treating Germany as a single economic unit with some central administrative departments, these plans failed. The turning point came in 1948, when the Soviets withdrew from the Four Power governing bodies and blockaded Berlin. Until May 1949, West Berlin was kept supplied only by an Allied airlift.

Political Developments in West Germany

The United States and the United Kingdom moved

to establish a nucleus for a future German government by creating a central Economic Council for
their two zones. The F.R.G. quickly progressed toward fuller sovereignty and association with its European neighbors and the Atlantic community. The
Allies stationed troops within the F.R.G. for NATO
defense, pursuant to stationing and status-of-forces
agreements.

Political Developments in East Germany

In the Soviet zone, the Social Democratic Party
was forced to merge with the Communist Party in
1946 to form a new party, the Socialist Unity Party
(SED). The October 1946 elections resulted in coali-
tion governments in the five Laender (state) parlia-
ments with the SED as the undisputed leader. The
G.D.R. established the structures of a single-party,
centralized, communist state.

German Unification

The constant stream of east Germans fleeing to
West Germany placed great strains on F.R.G.-G.D.R.
relations in the 1950s. On August 13, 1961, the
G.D.R. began building a wall through the center of
Berlin to divide the city and slow the flood of refugees
to a trickle. The Berlin Wall became the symbol of the
east's political debility and the division of Europe.

During the summer of 1989, rapid changes took place in the G.D.R., which ultimately led to German unification. Growing numbers of east Germans emigrated to the F.R.G. via Hungary after the Hungarians decided not to use force to stop them. Thousands of east Germans also tried to reach the west by staging sit-ins at F.R.G. diplomatic facilities in other east European capitals. The exodus generated demands within the G.D.R. for political change, and mass demonstrations in several cities—particularly in Leipzig—continued to grow. On October 7, Soviet leader Mikhail Gorbachev visited Berlin to celebrate the 40th anniversary of the establishment of the G.D.R. and urged the east German leadership to pursue reform.

On November 4, a demonstration in East Berlin drew as many as 1 million east Germans. Finally, on November 9, the Berlin Wall was opened, and east Germans were allowed to travel freely. Thousands poured through the wall into the western sectors of Berlin, and on November 12, the G.D.R. began dismantling it. On March 18, 1990, the first free elections were held in the G.D.R. Formal political union occurred on October 3, 1990. On December 2, 1990, all-German elections were held for the first time since 1933.

Eltz

Neptune Fountain And St. Mary's Church

Hints on Pronunciation

If you have studied German before, you may not need additional practice in pronunciation. However, unless you have had a chance to try out your German and know that you are understood without

Brandenburg Gate, Berlin

any difficulty, you had better do a little practicing.

All the words and phrases in this *Guide* are written both in German spelling and in a simplified spelling which you read like English. (Don't use the German spelling, the one given in parentheses, unless you have studied German before.) *Read the simplified spelling as though it were English.* Each letter or combination of letters is used for the sound it usually stands for in English and it *always* stands for that sound. Thus, *oo* is always pronounced as it is in *too, boot, tooth, roost,* never as anything else. Say these words and then pronounce the vowel sound by itself. That is the sound you must use every time you see *oo* in the *Pronunciation* column. If you should use some other sound—for example, the sound of *oo* in *blood*—you may be misunderstood.

Syllables that are accented, that is, pronounced louder than others, are written in capital letters. Curved lines (‿) are used to show sounds that are pronounced together without any break; for example, *P‿FEN-nik* meaning "pfennig," *P‿FEF-fer* meaning "pepper."

Special Points

AY	as in *may*, *say*, *play* but don't drawl it the way we do in English. Example: *TAY* meaning "tea."
O or *OH*	as in *go*, *so*, *oh*, *note*, *joke* but don't drawl it the way we do in English. Example: *VO* meaning "where."
AI	as in *aisle* or *ice*. Example: *AINSS* meaning "one."
EW	stands for a sound we do not have in English. To make it you round your lips as though to say the *oo* in *boo* and at the same time say the *ee* in *bee*. Example: *guh-MEW-zuh* meaning "vegetables."
ER	stands for a sound somewhat like the one in *her* except that you round your lips as you make the sound. Example: *TSVERLF* meaning "twelve."
KH	stands for a sound something like the one you make when you clear your throat. Example: *NAHKH* meaning "toward."

Memory Key

AY	as in *day* but not so drawled.
O or *OH*	as in *go* but not so drawled.
AI	as in *aisle* or *ice*.
EW	for the sound in *bee* said with the lips rounded.
ER	for the sound in *her* said with the lips rounded.
KH	for a sound which is like the one you make when you clear your throat.

Schiller Memorial And Schauspielhaus Theater

Leipzig's Renovated City Hall

USEFUL WORDS AND PHRASES

GREETINGS AND GENERAL PHRASES

English	*Pronunciation and German Spelling*
Good morning	*GOO-ten MAWR-gen* (Guten Morgen)
Good day	*GOO-ten TAHK* (Guten Tag)

ow as in *now; ai* as in *aisle* or *ice*

7

English	Pronunciation and German Spelling
Good evening	*GOO-ten AH-bent* (Guten Abend)
How are you?	*vee GAYT ess ee-nen?* (Wie geht es Ihnen?)
Sir	*main HAYR* (mein Herr)
Madam	*G⏝NAY-dig-uh FROW* (gnädige Frau)
Miss	*G⏝NAY-dig-ess FROY-lain* (gnädiges Fräulein)

When you address a person by name you say:

Mr. Schmidt	*HAYR SHMIT* (Herr Schmidt)
Mrs. Schmidt	*FROW SHMIT* (Frau Schmidt)
Miss Schmidt	*FROY-lain SHMIT* (Fräulein Schmidt)
Please	*BIT-tuh* (Bitte)
Excuse me	*fayr-TSAI-oong* (Verzeihung)
Thank you	*DAN-kuh* (Danke)

When someone thanks you, you answer with the word for "please."

Please	*BIT-tuh* (Bitte)
Yes	*YA* (Ja)
No	*NAIN* (Nein)

ow as in *now; ai* as in *aisle* or *ice*

8

English	Pronunciation and German Spelling
Do you under-stand?	*fer-SHTAY-en zee?* (Verstehen Sie?)
I understand	*ish fer-SHTAY-uh* (Ich verstehe)
I don't under-stand	*ish fer-SHTAY-uh nisht* (Ich verstehe nicht)
Speak slowly	*SHPRESH-en zee LAHNK-zahm* (Sprechen Sie langsam)
Please repeat	*BIT-tuh vee-der-HO-len zee* (Bitte wiederholen Sie)

LOCATION

When you need directions to get somewhere you use the phrase "Where is?" and then add the words you need.

Where is	*VO IST* (Wo ist)
a restaurant	*ain ress-to-RAHNG* (ein Restaurant)
Where is a restaurant?	*VO ist ain ress-to-RAHNG?* (Wo ist ein Restaurant?)
a hotel	*ain ho-TEL* (ein Hotel)
Where is a hotel?	*VO ist ain ho-TEL?* (Wo ist ein Hotel?)

ow as in *now; ai* as in *aisle* or *ice*

9

English	Pronunciation and German Spelling
a railroad station	*ain BAHN-hohf* (ein Bahnhof)
Where is a railroad station?	*VO ist ain BAHN-hohf?* (Wo ist ein Bahnhof?)
a toilet	*ai-nuh twa-LET-tuh* (eine Toilette)
Where is a toilet?	*VO ist ai-nuh twa-LET-tuh?* (Wo ist eine Toilette?)

DIRECTIONS

The answer to your question "Where is such and such?" may be "To the right" or "To the left" or "Straight ahead," so you need to know these phrases.

To the right   *nahkh RESHTS* (nach rechts)

To the left   *nahkh LINKS* (nach links)

In the word *NAHKH* you heard a sound you must practice. It is written in your *Language Guide* as *kh*. Listen to the word again and repeat: *NAHKH, NAHKH*.

Straight ahead   *guh-RA-duh-OWSS* (geradeaus)

It is sometimes useful to say "Please show me."

ow as in *now; ai* as in *aisle* or *ice*

English	Pronunciation and German Spelling

Please show me *BIT-tuh TSAI-gen zee meer*   (Bitte zeigen
Sie mir)

If you are driving and ask the distance to another town, it will be given you in kilometers, not miles.

Kilometer   *kee-lo-MAY-ter*   (Kilometer)

One kilometer equals 5/8 of a mile.

NUMBERS

You need to know the numbers.

One	*AINSS*	eins
Two	*TSVAI*	zwei
Three	*DRAI*	drei
Four	*FEER*	vier
Five	*FEWNF*	fünf
Six	*ZEKS*	sechs
Seven	*ZEE-ben*	sieben
Eight	*AHKHT*	acht
Nine	*NOYN*	neun
Ten	*TSAYN*	zehn

ow as in *now; ai* as in *aisle* or *ice*

11

English	Pronunciation and German Spelling	
Eleven	*ELF*	elf
Twelve	*TSVERLF*	zwölf

Notice the sound of *er* in the last word. Listen to the word again and repeat: *TSVERLF, TSVERLF.* We don't have this sound in English, but the sound we have in "her" is close to it. Round your lips as though you were pronouncing the "o" in *go*, and at the same time say the *er* in *her*. Try just the sound again: *er, er*.

Thirteen	*DRAI-tsayn*	dreizehn
Fourteen	*FEER-tsayn*	vierzehn
Fifteen	*FEWNF-tsayn*	fünfzehn
Sixteen	*ZESH-tsayn*	sechzehn
Seventeen	*ZEEP-tsayn*	siebzehn
Eighteen	*AHKH-tsayn*	achtzehn
Nineteen	*NOYN-tsayn*	neunzehn
Twenty	*TSVAHN-tsik*	zwanzig

To say "twenty-one," "twenty-two," etc. you say in German "one and twenty," "two and twenty," etc.

ow as in *now; ai* as in *aisle* or *ice*

The Old Museum And Plaza, Berlin

English	Pronunciation and German Spelling	
Twenty-one	*AIN-oont-tsvahn-tsik*	einundzwanzig
Twenty-two	*TSVAI-oont-tsvahn-tsik*	zweiundzwanzig
Thirty	*DRAI-sik*	dreissig
Forty	*FEER-tsik*	vierzig
Fifty	*FEWNF-tsik*	fünfzig
Sixty	*ZESH-tsik*	sechzig
Seventy	*ZEEP-tsik*	siebzig
Eighty	*AHKH-tsik*	achtzig
Ninety	*NOYN-tsik*	neunzig
Hundred	*HOON-dert*	hundert
Thousand	*TOW-zent*	tausend

WHAT'S THIS ?

When you want to know the name of something you can say "What's this?" or "What's that?" and point to the thing you mean.

English	Pronunciation and German Spelling
What is	*VAHSS IST* (Was ist)
this	*DEESS* (dies)
What's this?	*VAHSS ist DEESS?* (Was ist dies?)
What's that?	*VAHSS ist DAHSS?* (Was ist das?)

ASKING FOR THINGS

When you want something, use the phrase "I want" and then add the name of the thing wanted.   Always use "Please"—*BIT-tuh*.

I want	*ish MERSH-tuh* (Ich möchte)
cigarettes	*tsee-ga-RET-ten* (Zigaretten)
I want cigarettes	*ish MERSH-tuh tsee-ga-RET-ten* (Ich möchte Zigaretten)
to eat	*ESS-sen* (essen)
I want to eat	*ish MERSH-tuh ESS-sen* (Ich möchte essen)

ow as in *now; ai* as in *aisle* or *ice*

Here are the words for some of the things you may require.

English	Pronunciation and German Spelling
drinking water	*TRINK-vahss-ser* (Trinkwasser)
bread	*BROHT* (Brot)
butter	*BOOT-ter* (Butter)
eggs	*AI-er* (Eier)
cheese	*KAY-zuh* (Käse)
meat	*FLAISH* (Fleisch)
pork	*SHVAI-nuh-flaish* (Schweinefleisch)
mutton	*HAHM-mel-flaish* (Hammelfleisch)
veal	*KAHLP-flaish* (Kalbfleisch)
beef	*RINT-flaish* (Rindfleisch)
chicken	*HOON* (Huhn)
fish	*FISH* (Fisch)
soup	*ZOOP-puh* (Suppe)
vegetables	*guh-MEW-zuh* (Gemüse)

You have just heard another sound you must practice. It is written in your *Guide* as *ew*. Listen to the

ow as in *now; ai* as in *aisle* or *ice*

15

word again and repeat: *guh-MEW-zuh*, *guh-MEW-zuh*.
To make this sound you round your lips as though
to say *oo* but say *ee* instead. Try just the sound again:
ew, ew.

English	*Pronunciation and German Spelling*
potatoes	*kar-TAWF-feln* (Kartoffeln)
beets	*RO-tuh REW-ben* (rote Rüben)
beans	*BO-nen* (Bohnen)
cabbage	*KOHL* (Kohl)
salad	*za-LAHT* (Salat)
fruit	*OHPST* (Obst)
milk	*MILSH* (Milch)
salt	*ZAHLTS* (Salz)
pepper	*P‿FEF-fer* (Pfeffer)
sugar	*TSOOK-ker* (Zucker)
chocolate	*sho-ko-LA-duh* (Schokolade)
tea	*TAY* (Tee)
coffee	*KAHF-fay* (Kaffee)
a cup of coffee	*ai-nuh TAHSS-suh KAHF-fay* (eine Tasse Kaffee)
wine	*VAIN* (Wein)

ow as in *now;* *ai* as in *aisle* or *ice*

English	Pronunciation and German Spelling
beer	*BEER* (Bier)
a glass of beer	*ain GLAHSS BEER* (ein Glas Bier)
tobacco	*TA-bahk* (Tabak)
matches	*SHTRAISH-herl-tser* (Streichhölzer)

MONEY

To find out how much things cost, you say:

How much	*vee-FEEL*	Wieviel
costs	*KAWSS-tet*	kostet
that	*DAHSS*	das

| How much does that cost? | *vee-feel KAWSS-tet DAHSS?* | (Wieviel kostet das?) |

TIME

When you want to know what time it is, you say really "How late is it?"

ow as in *now; ai* as in *aisle* or *ice*

English	Pronunciation and German Spelling

What time is it? *vee SHPAYT ist ess?*   (Wie spät ist es?)

Two o'clock   *TSVAI OOR*   (zwei Uhr)

Ten past two   *TSAYN nahkh TSVAI*   (zehn nach Zwei)

Quarter past five   *FEER-tel nahkh FEWNF*   (viertel nach Fünf)

"Half past six" is "six o'clock thirty" or "half seven."

Half past six   *ZEKS oor DRAI-sik*   (sechs Uhr dreissig) *or HAHLP ZEE-ben*   (halb Sieben)·

"A quarter of eight" is "three quarters eight."

Quarter of eight   *DRAI-feer-tel AHKHT*   (dreiviertel Acht)

"Five minutes to nine" is "five minutes before nine."

Five minutes to nine   *FEWNF mee-NOO-ten for NOYN*   (fünf Minuten vor Neun)

For the hours after 12 noon it is customary to say "thirteen o'clock"—*DRAI-tsayn OOR*, and so on, just as we do in the Army.

ow as in now; ai as in aisle or ice

If you want to know when a movie starts or when a train leaves, you say:

English	Pronunciation and German Spelling
When	*VAHN* (Wann)
begins	*buh-GINT* (beginnt)
the movie	*dahss KEE-no* (das Kino)
When does the movie start?	*VAHN buh-GINT dahss KEE-no?* (Wann beginnt das Kino?)
leaves	*GAYT* (geht)
the train	*dayr TSOOK* (der Zug)
When does the train leave?	*vahn GAYT dayr TSOOK?* (Wann geht der Zug?)
Yesterday	*GESS-tern* (gestern)
Today	*HOY-tuh* (heute)
Tomorrow	*MAWR-gen* (morgen)

The days of the week are:

Sunday	*ZAWN-tahk*	(Sonntag)
Monday	*MOHN-tahk*	(Montag)
Tuesday	*DEENSS-tahk*	(Dienstag)
Wednesday	*MIT-vawkh*	(Mittwoch)

ow as in *now; ai* as in *aisle* or *ice*

19

English	Pronunciation and German Spelling
Thursday	*DAWN-nerss-tahk* (Donnerstag)
Friday	*FRAI-tahk* (Freitag)
Saturday	*ZAMSS-tahk* (Samstag)
	or ZAWN-ah-bent (Sonnabend)

OTHER USEFUL PHRASES

The following phrases will be useful.

What is your name?	*VEE HAI-sen zee?* (Wie heissen Sie?)
My name is___	*ish HAI-suh___* (Ich heisse___)
How do you say *table* (or anything else) in German?	*vahss ZA-gen zee fewr* table *owf DOYTSH?* (Was sagen Sie für *table* auf Deutsch?)
I am an American	*ish bin ah-may-ree-KA-ner* (Ich bin Amerikaner)
Please help me	*BIT-tuh HEL-fen zee meer* (Bitte helfen Sie mir)
Where is the nearest town?	*VO ist dee NAYSH-stuh AWRT-shaft?* (Wo ist die nächste Ortschaft?)
Good-by	*owf VEE-der-zayn* (Auf Wiedersehen)

ow as in *now; ai* as in *aisle* or *ice*

ADDITIONAL EXPRESSIONS

English	*Pronunciation and German Spelling*
I am hungry	*ish HA-buh HOONG-er* (Ich habe Hunger)
I am thirsty	*ish HA-buh DOORST* (Ich habe Durst)
Halt! *or* **Stop!**	*HAHLT!* (Halt!)
Come here!	*KAWM-men zee HAYR!* (Kommen Sie her!)
Quickly	*SHNEL* (schnell)
Come quickly!	*KAWM-men zee SHNEL!* (Kommen Sie schnell!)
Go quickly!	*GAY-en zee SHNEL!* (Gehen Sie schnell!)
Help!	*HIL-fuh!* (Hilfe!)
Bring help!	*HO-len zee HIL-fuh!* (Holen Sie Hilfe!)
I am lost	*ish HA-buh mish fayr-LOW-fen* (Ich habe mich verlaufen)
I will pay you	*ish VAYR-duh EE-nen GELT GAY-ben* (Ich werde Ihnen Geld geben)
Where is the town?	*VO IST dee SHTAHT?* (Wo ist die Stadt?)

ow as in *now; ai* as in *aisle* or *ice*

English	Pronunciation and German Spelling
Where is it?	*VO IST ess?* (Wo ist es?)
How far is it?	*vee VAIT ist ess?* (Wie weit ist es?)
Which way is north?	*VO ist NAWR-den?* (Wo ist Norden?)
Which is the road to___?	*VO ist dayr VAYK nahkh___?* (Wo ist der Weg nach___?)
Draw me a map	*TSAISH-nen zee meer ai-nuh KAR-tuh* (Zeichnen Sie mir eine Karte)
Take me there	*BRIN-gen zee mish dawrt HIN* (Bringen Sie mich dort hin)
Take me to a doctor	*BRIN-gen zee mish tsoo AI-nem ARTST* (Bringen Sie mich zu einem Arzt)
Take me to a hospital	*BRIN-gen zee mish tsoo AI-nem la-tsa-RET* (Bringen Sie mich zu einem Lazarett)
Danger!	*guh-FAR!* (Gefahr!)
Watch out!	*OWF-pahss-sen!* (Aufpassen!)
Gas!	*GAHSS!* (Gas!)
Take cover!	*DEK-koong!* (Deckung!)
Wait a moment!	*VAR-ten zee ai-nen OW-gen-blik!* (Warten Sie einen Augenblick!)

ow as in *now; ai* as in *aisle* or *ice*

FILL-IN SENTENCES

In this section you will find a number of sentences, each containing a blank space which can be filled in with any one of the words in the list that follows. For example, to say "Where can I get some soap?" look for the phrase "Where can I get___?" in the English column and find the German expression given beside it: *VO kahn ish___buh-KAWM-men.* Then look for "soap" in the list that follows; the German word is *ZAI-fuh.* Put the word for "soap" in the blank space and you get *VO kahn ish ZAI-fuh buh-KAWM-men?*

English	*Pronunciation and German Spelling*
I want___	*ish MERSH-tuh___* (Ich möchte___)
We want___	*veer MERSH-ten___* (Wir möchten___)
Give me___	*GAY-ben zee meer___* (Geben Sie mir___)
Bring me___	*BRIN-gen zee meer___* (Bringen Sie mir___)
Get me___	*HO-len zee meer___* (Holen Sie mir___)
Where can I get___?	*VO kahn ish___ buh-KAWM-men?* (Wo kann ich___ bekommen?)
I have___	*ish HA-buh___* (Ich habe___)
We have___	*veer HA-ben___* (Wir haben___)
Have you___?	*HA-ben zee___?* (Haben Sie___?)

ow as in *now; ai* as in *aisle* or *ice*

Two historic castles on Rhine River

English	Pronunciation and German Spelling
	EXAMPLE
I want___	*ish MERSH-tuh___* (Ich möchte___)
food	*ET-vahss tsoo ESS-sen* (etwas zu essen)
I want food	*ish MERSH-tuh ET-vahss tsoo ESS-sen* (Ich möchte etwas zu essen)
apples	*EP-fel* (Äpfel)
bacon	*SHPEK* (Speck)
beefsteak	*BEEF-shtayk* (Beefsteak)
boiled water	*AHP-guh-kawkh-tess VAHSS-ser* (abgekochtes Wasser)

English	Pronunciation and German Spelling
carrots	*GEL-buh REW-ben* (gelbe Rüben)
cucumbers	*GOOR-ken* (Gurken)
grapes	*TROW-ben* (Trauben)
ham	*SHIN-ken* (Schinken)
a meal	*ai-nuh MAHL-tsait* (eine Mahlzeit)
onions	*TSVEE-beln* (Zwiebeln)
oranges	*ahp-fel-ZEE-nen* (Apfelsinen)
peas	*AYRP-sen* (Erbsen)
rice	*RAISS* (Reis)
spinach	*shpee-NAHT* (Spinat)
tangerines	*mahn-da-REE-nen* (Mandarinen)
turnips	*VAI-suh REW-ben* (weisse Rüben)

a cup	*ai-nuh TAHSS-suh* (eine Tasse)
a fork	*ai-nuh GA-bel* (eine Gabel)
a glass	*ain GLAHSS* (ein Glas)
a knife	*ain MESS-ser* (ein Messer)
a plate	*ai-nen TEL-ler* (einen Teller)

ow as in *now; ai* as in *aisle* or *ice*

English	Pronunciation and German Spelling
a spoon	*ai-nen LERF-fel* (einen Löffel)
a bed	*ain BET* (ein Bett)
bedding	*BET-tsoyk* (Bettzeug)
blankets	*DEK-ken* (Decken)
a mattress	*ai-nuh ma-TRA-tsuh* (eine Matratze)
a pillow	*ain KISS-sen* (ein Kissen)
a room	*ain TSIM-mer* (ein Zimmer)
sheets	*BET-la-ken* (Bettlaken)
cigars	*tsee-GAR-ren* (Zigarren)
a pipe	*ai-nuh P⌣FAI-fuh* (eine Pfeife)
pipe tobacco	*P⌣FAI-fen-ta-bahk* (Pfeifentabak)
ink	*TIN-tuh* (Tinte)
a pen	*ai-nen FAY-der-hahl-ter* (einen Federhalter,
a pencil	*ai-nen BLAI-shtift* (einen Bleistift)
a comb	*ai-nen KAHM* (einen Kamm)
hot water	*HAI-sess VAHSS-ser* (heisses Wasser)

ow as in *now; ai* as in *aisle* or *ice*

English	Pronunciation and German Spelling
a razor	*ai-nen ra-ZEER-ahp-pa-raht* (einen Rasierapparat)
razor blades	*ra-ZEER-kling-en* (Rasierklingen)
a shaving brush	*ai-nen ra-ZEER-pin-zel* (einen Rasierpinsel)
shaving soap	*ra-ZEER-zai-fuh* (Rasierseife)
soap	*ZAI-fuh* (Seife)
a toothbrush	*ai-nuh TSAHN-bewr-stuh* (eine Zahnbürste)
tooth paste	*TSAHN-kraym* (Zahncreme)
a towel	*ain HAHN-tookh* (ein Handtuch)
a handkerchief	*ain TA-shen-tookh* (ein Taschentuch)
a raincoat	*ai-nen RAY-gen-mahn-tel* (einen Regenmantel)
a shirt	*ain HEMT* (ein Hemd)
shoe laces	*SHNEWR-zen-kel* (Schnürsenkel)
shoe polish	*SHOO-kraym* (Schuhcreme)
shoes	*SHOO-uh* (Schuhe)
undershirt	*OON-ter-hemt* (Unterhemd)
undershorts	*OON-ter-ho-zen* (Unterhosen)

ow as in *now; ai* as in *aisle* or *ice*

English	Pronunciation and German Spelling
underwear	*OON-ter-vesh-shuh* (Unterwäsche)
buttons	*KNERP-fuh* (Knöpfe)
a needle	*ai-nuh NA-del* (eine Nadel)
pins	*SHTEK-na-deln* (Stecknadeln)
safety pins	*ZISH-sher-haits-na-deln* (Sicherheitsnadeln)
thread	*FA-den* (Faden)
aspirin	*ah-spee-REEN* (Aspirin)
a bandage	*ai-nuh BIN-duh* (eine Binde)
cotton	*VAHT-tuh* (Watte)
a disinfectant	*ain dess-in-fekts-YOHNSS-mit-tel* (ein Desinfektionsmittel)

Marksburg Castle Along The Rhine

English	Pronunciation and German Spelling
iodine	*YOHT* (Jod)
a laxative	*ain AHP-fewr-mit-tel* (ein Abführmittel)

I want to___	*ish MERSH-tuh*___ (Ich möchte___)

EXAMPLE

I want to___	*ish MERSH-tuh*___ (Ich möchte___)
eat	*ESS-sen* (essen)
I want to eat	*ish MERSH-tuh ESS-sen* (Ich möchte essen)

buy it	*ess KOW-fen* (es kaufen)
drink	*TRIN-ken* (trinken)
have my clothes washed	*mai-nuh ZA-khen VA-shen lahss-sen* (meine Sachen waschen lassen)
rest	*mish OWSS-roo-en* (mich ausruhen)
sleep	*SHLA-fen* (schlafen)
take a bath	*BA-den* (baden)
wash up	*mish VA-shen* (mich waschen)

ow as in *now;* *ai* as in *aisle* or *ice*

29

When you want a haircut or shave you say:

Haircut, please!   *BIT-tuh HA-ruh-shnai-den!*   (Bitte, Haareschneiden!)

Shave, please!   *BIT-tuh ra-ZEE-ren!*   (Bitte, Rasieren!)

Where is___?   *VO ist___?*   (Wo ist___?)

EXAMPLE

Where is___?	*VO ist___?*	(Wo ist___?)
a barber	*ain free-ZER*	(ein Friseur)
Where is a barber?	*VO ist ain free-ZER?*	(Wo ist ein Friseur?)
a bridge	*ai-nuh BREWK-kuh*	(eine Brücke)
a bus	*ain AWM-nee-booss*	(ein Omnibus)
a church	*ai-nuh KEER-shuh*	(eine Kirche)
a clothing store	*ain KLAI-der-la-den*	(ein Kleiderladen)
a dentist	*ain TSAHN-artst*	(ein Zahnarzt)
a doctor	*ain ARTST*	(ein Arzt)
a drugstore	*ai-nuh dro-gay-REE*	(eine Drogerie)
a fountain (or well)	*ain BROON-nen*	(ein Brunnen)
a garage	*ai-nuh ga-RA-shuh*	(eine Garage)
a grocery store	*ain LAY-benss-mit-tel-guh-SHEFT*	(ein Lebensmittelgeschäft)
a hospital	*ain la-tsa-RET*	(ein Lazarett)

English	Pronunciation and German Spelling
a house	*ain HOWSS* (ein Haus)
a laundry	*ai-nuh vesh-shuh-RAI* (eine Wascherei)
a mechanic	*ain may-SHA-nee-ker* (ein Mechaniker)
a pharmacy	*ai-nuh ah-po-TAY-kuh* (eine Apotheke)
a policeman	*ain po-lee-TSIST* (ein Polizist)
a porter	*ain guh-PAYK-tray-ger* (ein Gepäckträger)
a shoemaker	*ain SHOO-ster* (ein Schuster)
a (natural) spring	*ai-nuh KVEL-luh* (eine Quelle)
a tailor	*ain SHNAI-der* (ein Schneider)
a telephone	*ain tay-lay-FOHN* (ein Telephon)
a workman	*ain AR-bai-ter* (ein Arbeiter)
the camp	*dahss TROOP-pen-la-ger* (das Truppenlager)
the city	*dee SHTAHT* (die Stadt)
the highway	*dee LAHNT-shtra-suh* (die Landstrasse)
the main street	*dee HOWPT-shtra-suh* (die Hauptstrasse)
the market	*dayr MARKT* (der Markt)
the nearest town	*dee NAYSH-stuh AWRT-shaft* (die nächste Ortschaft)
the police station	*dahss po-lee-TSAI-ahmt* (das Polizeiamt)
the post office	*dahss PAWST-ahmt* (das Postamt)

Classic Facade, Wittenberg

Harburg

33

English	Pronunciation and German Spelling
the railroad	*dee AI-zen-bahn* (die Eisenbahn)
the river	*dayr FLOOSS* (der Fluss)
the road	*dayr VAYK* (der Weg)
the telegraph window (in post office)	*dayr tay-lay-GRAHM-shahl-ter* (der Telegrammschalter)

_____

I am___	*ish bin___*	(Ich bin___)
He is___	*ayr ist___*	(Er ist___)
We are___	*veer zint___*	(Wir sind___)
They are___	*zee zint___*	(Sie sind___)
Are you___?	*zint zee___?*	(Sind Sie___?)

EXAMPLE

I am___	*ish bin___*	(Ich bin___)
sick	*KRAHNK*	(krank)
I am sick	*ish bin KRAHNK*	(Ich bin krank)
tired	*MEW-duh*	(müde)
wounded	*fer-VOON-det*	(verwundet)

_____

Is it___?	*ist ess___?*	(Ist es___?)
It is___	*ess ist___*	(Es ist___)
It is not___	*ess ist nisht___*	(Es ist nicht___)

34

English	Pronunciation and German Spelling
That is___	*dahss ist___* (Das ist___)
This is___	*deess ist___* (Dies ist___)
That is too___	*dahss ist tsoo___* (Das ist zu___)
That is very___	*dahss ist zayr___* (Das ist sehr___)

EXAMPLE

It is not___	*ess ist nisht___* (Es ist nicht___ gut)	
good	*GOOT*	
It is not good	*ess ist nisht GOOT* (Es ist nicht gut)	
bad	*SHLESHT* (schlecht)	
expensive	*TOY-er* (teuer)	
large	*GROHSS* (gross)	
small	*KLAIN* (klein)	
clean	*ZOW-ber* (sauber)	
dirty	*SHMOO-tsik* (schmutzig)	
cold	*KAHLT* (kalt)	
hot	*HAISS* (heiss)	
few	*VAY-nik* (wenig)	
much	*FEEL* (viel)	
enough	*guh-NOOK* (genug)	
far	*VAIT* (weit)	
near	*NA-huh* (nahe)	
here	*HEER* (hier)	
there	*DAWRT* (dort)	

Reichstag Building

IMPORTANT SIGNS

German	English
Halt!	Stop!
Langsam!	Go slow!
Gefahr!	Danger!
Einbahnstrasse	One Way Street
Einbahnverkehr	One Way Traffic
Keine Durchfahrt	No Thoroughfare
Rechts fahren	Keep To The Right
Strasse im Bau	Road Under Construction
Kurve	Dangerous Curve
Kreuzung	Dangerous Crossing
Bahnübergang	Grade Crossing
Parken verboten	No Parking
Kein Zutritt	No Admittance
Frauen *or* Damen	Women
Männer *or* Herren	Men
Nichtraucher *or* Rauchen verboten	No Smoking
Eingang	Entrance
Ausgang	Exit

ALPHABETICAL
WORD LIST

English	Pronunciation and German Spelling

A

a
    ain (ein)
  or ain-en (einen)
  or ain-uh (eine)

am

 I am___ *ish BIN___* (Ich bin___)

American *ah-may-ree-KA-ner* (Amerikaner)

 I am an *ish BIN ah-may-ree-KA-ner*
  American   (Ich bin Amerikaner)

and   *oont* (und)

apples   *EP-fel* (Äpfel)

are   *zint* (sind)

 Are you___? *zint zee___?* (Sind Sie___?)

 They are___ *zee zint___* (Sie sind___)

 We are___ *veer zint___* (Wir sind___)

aspirin   *ah-spee-REEN* (Aspirin)

B

bacon	*SHPEK*	(Speck)
bad	*SHLESHT*	(schlecht)
bandage	*BIN-duh*	(Binde)
barber	*free-ZER*	(Friseur)
bath		
take a bath	*BA-den*	(baden)
beans	*BO-nen*	(Bohnen)
bed	*BET*	(Bett)
bedding	*BET-tsoyk*	(Bettzeug)
beef	*RINT-flaish*	(Rindfleisch)
beefsteak	*BEEF-shtayk*	(Beefsteak)
beer	*BEER*	(Bier)
a glass of beer	*ain GLAHSS BEER*	(ein Glas Bier)
beets	*RO-tuh REW-ben*	(rote Rüben)
begins	*buh-GINT*	(beginnt)
blankets	*DEK-ken*	(Decken)
boiled water	*AHP-guh-kawkh-tess VAHSS-ser*	(abgekochtes Wasser)
bread	*BROHT*	(Brot)

ow as in *now; ai* as in *aisle* or *ice*

English	Pronunciation and German Spelling
bridge	*BREWK-kuh* (Brücke)
bring	
Bring help!	*HO-len zee HIL-fuh!* (Holen Sie Hilfe!)
Bring me___	*BRIN-gen zee meer___* (Bringen Sie mir___)
bus	*AWM-nee-booss* (Omnibus)
butter	*BOOT-ter* (Butter)
buttons	*KNERP-fuh* (Knöpfe)
buy	
buy it	*ess KOW-fen* (es kaufen)

C

cabbage	*KOHL* (Kohl)
camp	*TROOP-pen-la-ger* (Truppenlager)
can	
Where can I get___?	*VO kahn ish___ buh-KAWM-men?* (Wo kann ich___ bekommen?)
carrots	*GEL-buh REW-ben* (gelbe Rüben)
cheese	*KAY-zuh* (Käse)
chicken	*HOON* (Huhn)

ow as in *now; ai* as in *aisle* or *ice*

Neuschwanstein Castle

English	Pronunciation and German Spelling
chocolate	*sho-ko-LA-duh* (Schokolade)
church	*KEER-shuh* (Kirche)
cigarettes	*tsee-ga-RET-ten* (Zigaretten)
cigars	*tsee-GAR-ren* (Zigarren)
city	*SHTAHT* (Stadt)
clean	*ZOW-ber* (sauber)
clothing store	*KLAI-der-la-den* (Kleiderladen)
coffee	*KAHF-fay* (Kaffee)
a cup of coffee	*ai-nuh TAHSS-suh KAHF-fay* (eine Tasse Kaffee)
cold	*KAHLT* (kalt)

ow as in *now; ai* as in *aisle* or *ice*   **41**

English	_Pronunciation and German Spelling_
comb	_KAHM_ (Kamm)
Come!	_KAWM-men zee!_ (Kommen Sie!)
Come here!	_KAWM-men zee HAYR!_ (Kommen Sie her!)
Come quickly!	_KAWM-men zee SHNEL!_ (Kommen Sie schnell!)
cost	_KAWST-et_ (kostet)
How much does that cost?	_vee-feel KAWSS-tet DAHSS?_ (Wieviel kostet das?)
cotton	_VAHT-tuh_ (Watte)
cover	
Take cover!	_DEK-koong!_ (Deckung!)
cucumbers	_GOOR-ken_ (Gurken)
cup	_TAHSS-suh_ (Tasse)
a cup of___	_ai-nuh TAHSS-suh____ (eine Tasse___)

D

Danger!	_guh-FAR!_ (Gefahr!)
day	_TAHK_ (Tag)
Good day	_GOO-ten TAHK_ (Guten Tag)

_ow_ as in _now; ai_ as in _aisle_ or _ice_

English	Pronunciation and German Spelling
dentist	*TSAHN-artst* (Zahnarzt)
dirty	*SHMOO-tsik* (schmutzig)
disinfectant	*dess-in-fekts-YOHNSS-mit-tel* (Desinfektionsmittel)
Do you understand?	*fer-SHTAY-en zee?* (Verstehen Sie?)
doctor	*ARTST* (Arzt)
Take me to a doctor	*BRIN-gen zee mish tsoo ai-nem ARTST* (Bringen Sie mich zu einem Arzt)
Draw me a map	*TSAISH-nen zee meer ai-nuh KAR-tuh* (Zeichnen Sie mir eine Karte)
drink	*TRIN-ken* (trinken)
drinking water	*TRINK-vahss-ser* (Trinkwasser)
drugstore	*dro-gay-REE* (Drogerie)

E

eat	*ESS-sen* (essen)
something to eat	*ET-vahss tsoo ESS-sen* (etwas zu essen)
I want to eat	*ish MERSH-tuh ESS-sen* (Ich möchte essen)
eggs	*AI-er* (Eier)
eight	*AHKHT* (acht)

ow as in *now; ai* as in *aisle* or *ice*

English	Pronunciation and German Spelling
eighteen	*AHKH-tsayn* (achtzehn)
eighty	*AHKH-tsik* (achtzig)
eleven	*ELF* (elf)
enough	*guh-NOOK* (genug)
Excuse me	*fayr-TSAI-oong* (Verzeihung)
evening	*AH-bent* (Abend)
Good evening	*GOO-ten AH-bent* (Guten Abend)
expensive	*TOY-er* (teuer)

F

far	*VAIT* (weit)
How far is it?	*vee VAIT ist ess?* (Wie weit ist es?)
Is it far?	*ist ess VAIT?* (Ist es weit?)
few	*VAY-nik* (wenig)
fifteen	*FEWNF-tsayn* (fünfzehn)
fifty	*FEWNF-tsik* (fünfzig)
fish	*FISH* (Fisch)
five	*FEWNF* (fünf)
food	*ET-vahss tsoo ESS-sen* (etwas zu essen)
fork	*GA-bel* (Gabel)
forty	*FEER-tsik* (vierzig)

ow as in *now; ai* as in *aisle* or *ice*

English	Pronunciation and German Spelling
fountain (well)	*BROON-nen* (Brunnen)
four	*FEER* (vier)
fourteen	*FEER-tsayn* (vierzehn)
Friday	*FRAI-tahk* (Freitag)
fruit	*OHPST* (Obst)

G

garage	*ga-RA-shuh* (Garage)
Gas!	*GAHSS!* (Gas!)
German	*DOYTSH* (Deutsch)
in German	*owf DOYTSH* (auf Deutsch)
get	
Get me___	*HO-len zee meer___* (Holen Sie mir___)
Where can I get___?	*VO kahn ish___buh-KAWM-men?* (Wo kann ich bekommen?)
Give me___	*GAY-ben zee meer___* (Geben Sie mir___)
glass	*GLAHSS* (Glas)
a glass of___	*ain GLAHSS___* (ein Glas___)

ow as in *now; ai* as in *aisle* or *ice*

English.	Pronunciation and German Spelling
Go!	*GAY-en zeel* (Gehen Sie!)
Go quickly!	*GAY-en zee SHNEL!* (Gehen Sie schnell!)
good	*GOOT* (gut)
Good day	*GOO-ten TAHK* (Guten Tag)
Good evening	*GOO-ten AH-bent* (Guten Abend)
Good morning	*GOO-ten MAWR-gen* (*Guten Morgen*)
Good-by	*owf VEE-der-zayn* (Auf Wiedersehen)
grapes	*TROW-ben* (Trauben)
grocery store	*LAY-benss-mit-tel-guh-SHEFT* (Lebensmittelgeschäft)

H

hair	*HAR* (Haar)
Haircut, please!	*BIT-tuh HA-ruh-shnai-den!* (Bitte, Haareschneiden!)
half	*HAHLP* (halb)
Halt!	*HAHLT!* (Halt!)
ham	*SHIN-ken* (Schinken)
handkerchief	*TA-shen-tookh* (Taschentuch)

ow as in *now; ai* as in *aisle* or *ice*

English	Pronunciation and German Spelling
have	
Have you___?	*HA-ben zee___?* (Haben Sie___?)
I have___	*ish HA-buh___* (Ich habe___)
We have___	*veer HA-ben___* (Wir haben___)
he	*ayr* (er)
He is___	*ayr ist___* (Er ist___)
Help!	*HIL-fuh!* (Hilfe!)
Bring help!	*HO-len zee HIL-fuh!* (Holen Sie Hilfe!)
Please help me	*BIT-tuh HEL-fen zee meer* (Bitte helfen Sie mir)
here	*HEER* (hier)
It is here	*ess ist HEER* (Es ist hier)
Come here!	*KAWM-men zee hayr!* (Kommen Sie her!)
highway	*LAHNT-shtra-suh* (Landstrasse)
hospital	*la-tsa-RET* (Lazarett)
Take me to a hospital	*BRIN-gen zee mish tsoo AI-nem la-tsa-RET* (Bringen Sie mich zu einem Lazarett)
hot	*HAISS* (heiss)
hot water	*HAI-sess VAHSS-ser* (heisses Wasser)
hotel	*ho-TEL* (Hotel)

ow as in *now; ai* as in *aisle* or *ice*

English	_Pronunciation and German Spelling_
Where is a hotel?	_VO ist ain ho-TEL?_ (Wo ist ein Hotel?)
house	_HOWSS_ (Haus)
how	_VEE_ (wie)
How are you?	_vee GAYT ess ee-nen?_ (Wie geht es Ihnen?)
How do you say _table_ in German?	_vahss ZA-gen zee fewr_ table _owf DOYTSH?_ (Was sagen Sie für _table_ auf Deutsch?)
How far is it?	_vee VAIT ist ess?_ (Wie weit ist es?)

_ow_ as in _now; ai_ as in _aisle_ or _ice_

Ettal Monastery, Bavaria

48

English	Pronunciation and German Spelling
How much does that cost?	*vee-feel KAWSS-tet DAHSS?* (Wieviel kostet das?)
hundred	*HOON-dert* (hundert)
hungry	
I am hungry	*ish HA-buh HOONG-er* (Ich habe Hunger)

I

I	*ish* (ich)
I am___	*ish bin___* (Ich bin___)
I have___	*ish HA-buh___* (Ich habe___)
I want___	*ish MERSH-tuh___* (Ich möchte___)
or I want to___	
in German	*owf DOYTSH* (auf Deutsch)
ink	*TIN-tuh* (Tinte)
iodine	*YOHT* (Jod)
is	*ist* (ist)
Is it___?	*IST ess___?* (Ist es___?)
It is___	*ess IST___* (Es ist___)
It is not___	*ess ist NISHT___* (Es ist nicht___)

ow as in *now; ai* as in *aisle* or *ice*

49

K

kilometer	*kee-lo-MAY-ter*	(Kilometer)
knife	*MESS-ser*	(Messer)

L

large	*GROHSS*	(gross)
laundry	*vesh-shuh-RAI*	(Wäscherei)
laxative	*AHP-fewr-mit-tel*	(Abführmittel)
leave	*GAYT*	(geht)

When does the train leave?   *vahn GAYT dayr TSOOK?*
(Wann geht der Zug?)

left	*LINKS*	(links)

To the left   *nahkh LINKS*   (nach links)

lost

I am lost   *ish HA-buh mish fayr-LOW-fen*
(Ich habe mich verlaufen)

M

madam	*G‿NAY-dig-uh FROW*	(gnädige Frau)
main street	*HOWPT-shtra-suh*	(Hauptstrasse)
map	*KAR-tuh*	(Karte)

ow as in *now; ai* as in *aisle* or *ice*

Castle Church Tower, Wittenburg

Linderhof

English	Pronunciation and German Spelling
Draw me a map	*TSAISH-nen zee meer ai-nuh KAR-tuh* (Zeichnen Sie mir eine Karte)
mark	*MARK* (Mark)
market	*MARKT* (Markt)
matches	*SHTRAISH-herl-tser* (Streichhölzer)
mattress	*ma-TRA-tsuh* (Matratze)
me	*mish* (mich)
or	*meer* (mir)
meal	*MAHL-tsait* (Mahlzeit)
meat	*FLAISH* (Fleisch)
mechanic	*may-SHA-nee-ker* (Mechaniker)
milk	*MILSH* (Milch)
Miss	*FROY-lain* (Fräulein)
or	*G⌣NAY-dig-ess FROY-lain* (gnädiges Fräulein)
Mister	*HAYR* (Herr)
Monday	*MOHN-tahk* (Montag)
morning	*MAWR-gen* (Morgen)
movie	*KEE-no* (Kino)
When does the movie start?	*VAHN buh-GINT dahss KEE-no?* (Wann beginnt das Kino?)

ow as in *now; ai* as in *aisle* or *ice*

English	Pronunciation and German Spelling
Mrs.	*FROW* (Frau)
much	*FEEL* (viel)
mutton	*HAHM-mel-flaish* (Hammelfleisch)

N

name	
My name is___	*ish HAI-suh___* (Ich heisse___)
What's your name?	*VEE HAI-sen zee?* (Wie heissen Sie?)
near	*NA-huh* (nahe)
the nearest town	*dee NAYSH-stuh AWRT-shaft* (die nächste Ortschaft)
needle	*NA-del* (Nadel)
nine	*NOYN* (neun)
nineteen	*NOYN-tsayn* (neunzehn)
ninety	*NOYN-tsik* (neunzig)
no	*NAIN* (nein)
north	*NAWR-den* (Norden)
Which way is north?	*VO ist NAWR-den?* (Wo ist Norden?)
not	*nisht* (nicht)

ow as in *now; ai* as in *aisle* or *ice*

O

one	*AINSS* (eins)
onions	*TSVEE-beln* (Zwiebeln)
oranges	*ahp-fel-ZEE-nen* (Apfelsinen)

P

pay

I will pay you *ish VAYR-duh EE-nen GELT GAY-ben*
(Ich werde Ihnen Geld geben)

peas	*AYRP-sen* (Erbsen)
pen	*FAY-der-hahl-ter* (Federhalter)
pencil	*BLAI-shtift* (Bleistift)
pepper	*P⌣FEF-fer* (Pfeffer)
pfennig	*P⌣FEN-nik* (Pfennig)
pharmacy	*ah-po-TAY-kuh* (Apotheke)
pillow	*KISS-sen* (Kissen)
pins	*SHTEK-na-deln* (Stecknadeln)
safety pins	*ZISH-sher-haits-na-deln* (Sicherheitsnadeln)

ow as in *now; ai* as in *aisle* or *ice*

English	Pronunciation and German Spelling
pipe	*P⌣FAI-fuh* (Pfeife)
pipe tobacco	*P⌣FAI-fen-ta-bahk* (Pfeifentabak)
plate	*TEL-ler* (Teller)
Please	*BIT-tuh* (Bitte)
police station	*po-lee-TSAI-ahmt* (Polizeiamt)
policeman	*po-lee-TSIST* (Polizist)
pork	*SHVAI-nuh-flaish* (Schweinefleisch)
porter	*guh-PAYK-tray-ger* (Gepäckträger)
post office	*PAWST-ahmt* (Postamt)
potatoes	*kar-TAWF-feln* (Kartoffeln)

Q

quickly	*SHNEL* (schnell)
Come quickly!	*KAWM-men zee SHNEL!* (Kommen Sie schnell!)
Go quickly!	*GAY-en zee SHNEL!* (Gehen Sie schnell!)

R

railroad	*AI-zen-bahn* (Eisenbahn)
railroad station	*BAHN-hohf* (Bahnhof)

ow as in *now; ai* as in *aisle* or *ice*

Spree River, Linden Bridge

English	Pronunciation and German Spelling
Where is a railroad station?	*VO ist ain BAHN-hohf?* (Wo ist ein Bahnhof?)
raincoat	*RAY-gen-mahn-tel* (Regenmantel)
razor	*ra-ZEER-ahp-pa-raht* (Rasierapparat)
razor blades	*ra-ZEER-kling-en* (Rasierklingen)
repeat	*vee-der-HO-len zeel* (Wiederholen Sie!)
Please repeat	*BIT-tuh vee-der-HO-len zee* (Bitte wiederholen Sie)
rest	
I want to rest	*ish MERSH-tuh mish OWSS-roo-en* (Ich möchte mich ausruhen)

English	Pronunciation and German Spelling
restaurant	*ress-to-RAHNG* (Restaurant)
Where is a restaurant?	*VO ist ain ress-to-RAHNG?* (Wo ist ein Restaurant?)
rice	*RAISS* (Reis)
right	*RESHTS* (rechts)
To the right	*nahkh RESHTS* (nach rechts)
river	*FLOOSS* (Fluss)
road	*VAYK* (Weg)
Which is the road to___?	*VO ist dayr VAYK nahkh___?* (Wo ist der Weg nach___?)
room	*TSIM-mer* (Zimmer)

S

safety pins	*ZISH-sher-haits-na-deln* (Sicherheitsnadeln)
salad	*za-LAHT* (Salat)
salt	*ZAHLTS* (Salz)
Saturday	*ZAMSS-tahk* (Samstag) *or* *ZAWN-ah-bent* (Sonnabend)
(to) say	*ZA-gen* (sagen)

ow as in *now; ai* as in *aisle* or *ice*

English	Pronunciation and German Spelling
How do you say *table* in German?	*vahss ZA-gen zee fewr* table *owf DOYTSH?* (Was sagen Sie für *table* auf Deutsch?)
seven	*ZEE-ben* (sieben)
seventeen	*ZEEP-tsayn* (siebzehn)
seventy	*ZEEP-tsik* (siebzig)
shave	
Shave, please!	*BIT-tuh ra-ZEE-ren!* (Bitte, Rasieren!)
shaving brush	*ra-ZEER-pin-zel* (Rasierpinsel)
shaving soap	*ra-ZEER-zai-fuh* (Rasierseife)
she	*zee* (sie)
sheets	*BET-la-ken* (Bettlaken)
shirt	*HEMT* (Hemd)
undershirt	*OON-ter-hemt* (Unterhemd)
shoemaker	*SHOO-ster* (Schuster)
shoes	*SHOO-uh* (Schuhe)
shoe laces	*SHNEWR-zen-kel* (Schnürsenkel)
shoe polish	*SHOO-kraym* (Schuhcreme)

ow as in *now; ai* as in *aisle* or *ice*

English	Pronunciation and German Spelling
show	
Please show me	*BIT-tuh TSAI-gen zee meer* (Bitte zeigen Sie mir)
sick	*KRAHNK* (krank)
sir	*main HAYR* (mein Herr)
six	*ZEKS* (sechs)
sixteen	*ZESH-tsayn* (sechzehn)
sixty	*ZESH-tsik* (sechzig)
sleep	*SHLA-fen* (schlafen)
slowly	*LAHNK-zahm* (langsam)
Speak slowly	*SPRESH-en zee LAHNK-zahm* (Sprechen Sie langsam,
small	*KLAIN* (klein,
soap	*ZAI-fuh* (Seife)
shaving soap	*ra-ZEER-zai-fuh* (Rasierseife)

Rhine River Castle, Bacharach

English	Pronunciation and German Spelling
soldiers	*zawl-DA-ten* (Soldaten)
soup	*ZOOP-puh* (Suppe)
speak	*SPRESH-en zeel* (Sprechen Sie!)
Speak slowly	*SPRESH-en zee LAHNK-zahm* (Sprechen Sie langsam)
spinach	*shpee-NAHT* (Spinat)
spoon	*LERF-fel* (Löffel)
(natural) spring	*KVEL-luh* (Quelle)
start	*buh-GINT* (beginnt)
When does the movie start?	*VAHN buh-GINT dahss KEE-no?* (Wann beginnt das Kino?)
station	
police station	*po-lee-TSAI-ahmt* (Polizeiamt)
railroad station	*BAHN-hohf* (Bahnhof)
Stop!	*HAHLT!* (Halt!)

ow as in *now;* *ai* as in *aisle* or *ice*

English	Pronunciation and German Spelling
store	
clothing store	*KLAI-der-la-den* (Kleiderladen)
drugstore	*dro-gay-REE* (Drogerie)
Straight ahead	*guh-RA-duh-OWSS* (geradeaus)
street	*SHTRA-suh* (Strasse)
main street	*HOWPT-shtra-suh* (Hauptstrasse)
sugar	*TSOOK-ker* (Zucker)
Sunday	*ZAWN-tahk* (Sonntag)

T

tailor	*SHNAI-der* (Schneider)
take	
Take cover!	*DEK-koong!* (Deckung!)
Take me to a doctor	*BRIN-gen zee mish tsoo AI-nem ARTST* (Bringen Sie mich zu einem Arzt)
Take me to a hospital	*BRIN-gen zee mish tsoo AI-nem la-tsa-RET* (Bringen Sie mich zu einem Lazarett)
Take me there	*BRIN-gen zee mish dawrt HIN* (Bringen Sie mich dort hin)

ow as in *now; ai* as in *aisle* or *ice*

Handel Statue At Halle

Cochem

English	Pronunciation and German Spelling
tangerines	*mahn-da-REE-nen* (Mandarinen)
tea	*TAY* (Tee)
telegraph window (in post office)	*tay-lay-GRAHM-shahl-ter* (Telegrammschalter)
telephone	*tay-lay-FOHN* (Telephon)
ten	*TSAYN* (zehn)
Thank you	*DAN-kuh* (Danke)
that	*dahss* (das)
What's that?	*VAHSS ist DAHSS?* (Was ist das?)
the	*dayr* (der)
	or dee (die)
	or dahss (das)
there	*DAWRT* (dort).
Take me there	*BRIN-gen zee mish dawrt HIN* (Bringen Sie mich dort hin)
they	*zee* (sie)
They are___	*zee zint___* (Sie sind___)
thirsty	
I am thirsty	*ish HA-buh DOORST* (Ich habe Durst)
thirteen	*DRAI-tsayn* (dreizehn)

ow as in *now; ai* as in *aisle* or *ice*

English	Pronunciation and German Spelling
thirty	*DRAI-sik* (dreissig)
this	*DEESS* (dies)
What's this?	*VAHSS ist DEESS?* (Was ist dies?)
thousand	*TOW-zent* (tausend)
thread	*FA-den* (Faden)
three	*DRAI* (drei)
Thursday	*DAWN-nerss-tahk* (Donnerstag)
time	
What time is it?	*vee SHPAYT ist ess?* (Wie spät ist es?)
tired	*MEW-duh* (müde)
tobacco	*TA-bahk* (Tabak)
today	*HOY-tuh* (heute)
toilet	*twa-LET-tuh* (Toilette)
Where is a toilet?	*VO ist ai-nuh twa-LET-tuh?* (Wo ist eine Toilette?)
tomorrow	*MAWR-gen* (morgen)
too	*tsoo* (zu)
toothbrush	*TSAHN-bewr-stuh* (Zahnbürste)
tooth paste	*TSAHN-kraym* (Zahncreme)

ow as in *now; ai* as in *aisle* or *ice*

English	Pronunciation and German Spelling
towel	*HAHN-tookh* (Handtuch)
town	*AWRT-shaft* (Ortschaft) *or SHTAHT* (Stadt)
the nearest town	*dee NAYSH-stuh AWRT-shaft* (die nächste Ortschaft)
train	*TSOOK* (Zug)
When does the train leave?	*vahn GAYT dayr TSOOK?* (Wann geht der Zug?)
Tuesday	*DEENSS-tahk* (Dienstag)
turnips	*VAI-suh REW-ben* (weisse Rüben)
twelve	*TSVERLF* (zwölf)
twenty	*TSVAHN-tsik* (zwanzig)
two	*TSVAI* (zwei)

U

undershirt	*OON-ter-hemt* (Unterhemd)
undershorts	*OON-ter-ho-zen* (Unterhosen)
understand	
Do you understand?	*fer-SHTAY-en zee?* (Verstehen Sie?)
I understand	*ish fer-SHTAY-uh* (Ich verstehe)

ow as in *now; ai* as in *aisle* or *ice*

English	Pronunciation and German Spelling
I don't understand	*ish fer-SHTAY-uh nisht* (Ich verstehe nicht)
underwear	*OON-ter-vesh-shuh* (Unterwäsche)

V

veal	*KAHLP-flaish* (Kalbfleisch)
vegetables	*guh-MEW-zuh* (Gemüse)
very	*zayr* (sehr)

W

Wait!	*VAR-ten zee!* (Warten Sie!)
Wait a moment!	*VAR ten zee ai-nen OW-gen-blik!* (Warten Sie einen Augenblick!)
want	
I want____ or I want to____	*ish MERSH-tuh____* (Ich möchte____)
We want____	*veer MERSH-ten____* (Wir möchten____)
wash	*VA-shen* (waschen)
I want to wash up	*ish MERSH-tuh mish VA-shen* (Ich möchte mich waschen)

ow as in *now; ai* as in *aisle* or *ice*

64

English	Pronunciation and German Spelling
I want to have my clothes washed	*ish MERSH-tuh mai-nuh ZA-khen VA-shen lahss-sen* (Ich möchte meine Sachen waschen lassen)
Watch out!	*OWF-pahss-sen!* (Aufpassen!)
water	*VAHSS-ser* (Wasser)
boiled water	*AHP-guh-kawkh-tess VAHSS-ser* (abgekochtes Wasser)
drinking water	*TRINK-vahss-ser* (Trinkwasser)
hot water	*HAI-sess VAHSS-ser* (heisses Wasser)
we	*veer* (wir)
We are___	*veer zint___* (Wir sind___)
We have___	*veer HA-ben___* (Wir haben___)
We want___	*veer MERSH-ten___* (Wir möchten___)
Wednesday	*MIT-vawkh* (Mittwoch)
welcome	
You're welcome	*BIT-tuh* (Bitte)
well	
I am well	*es GAYT meer GOOT* (Es geht mir gut)

ow as in *now;* *ai* as in *aisle* or *ice*

English	Pronunciation and German Spelling
well (for water)	*BROON-nen* (Brunnen)
what	*VAHSS* (was)
What's that?	*VAHSS ist DAHSS?* (Was ist das?)
What's this?	*VAHSS ist DEESS?* (Was ist dies?)
What is your name?	*VEE HAI-sen zee?* (Wie heissen Sie?)
What time is it?	*vee SHPAYT ist ess?* (Wie spät ist es?)
when	*VAHN* (wann)
When does the movie start?	*VAHN buh-GINT dahss KEE-no?* (Wann beginnt das Kino?)
When does the train leave?	*vahn GAYT dayr TSOOK?* (Wann geht der Zug?)
where	*VO* (wo)
Where is___?	*vo ist___?* (Wo ist___?)
Where are___?	*vo zint___?* (Wo sind___?)
Where can I get___?	*vo kahn ish___ buh-KAWM-men?* (Wo kann ich___ bekommen?)
wine	*VAIN* (Wein)

ow as in *now; ai* as in *aisle* or *ice*

Old Town's Romerberg Square, Frankfurt

English	Pronunciation and German Spelling
workman	*A R-bai-ter* (Arbeiter)
wounded	*fayr-VOON-det* (verwundet)

Y

yes	*YA* (ja)
yesterday	*GESS-tern* (gestern)
you	

Are you___? *sint zee___?* (Sind Sie___?)

Have you___? *HA-ben zee___?* (Haben Sie___?)

Wartburg Castle